£1   01.25

CANNIBAL VICTIMS SPEAK OUT!

and other astonishing press cuttings

CANNIBAL VICTIMS SPEAK OUT!

and other astonishing press cuttings

Edited by
MAT COWARD

With illustrations by
DAVID LYTTLETON

VICTOR GOLLANCZ
LONDON

This book is dedicated to the memory of my old friend Raf Negri, who loved a laugh, and gave me more of them than anyone I've ever known.

First published in Great Britain 1995
By Victor Gollancz
An imprint of the Cassell Group
Wellington House, 125 Strand,
London WC2R 0BB

A catalogue record for this book is available from the British Library.

ISBN 0 575 06163 4

Designed and typeset by
Fishtail Design

Printed and bound in Finland
by Werner Söderström Oy

ONTRODICTION

Ever since human beings learned to talk, they have been saying things they didn't intend to say – often with (to use the phrase immortalized by TV listings magazines) 'hilarious results'. The invention of printing, swiftly followed as it was by the invention of misprints, only made matters worse – and more permanent.

And for almost as long as the printed page has existed, there have been people like me, collecting and collating the mistakes of others – typos, bloopers, *double entendres*, accidental puns, absurd headlines and bizarre claims – and cruelly drawing attention to them, publicly displaying them for fun and profit.

It's a disgrace, really, when you think about it. Still, never mind, eh? Anyway, here it is, *Cannibal Victims Speak Out*, a colecshun off starnge noosepepper kuttings.

I would, by the way, like to apologize in advance for any errors which may appear in this book; as I'm sure you can appreciate, it's been an absolute bugger to priffrood.

MAT COWARD

DANGER!
GENIUS AT WORK

A Thai provincial governor has officially declared war on about 600 monkeys for destroying public property but refused to make public his tactics because 'it will leak out to the monkeys'.

Daily Telegraph

Jack Rains, a candidate for Governor of Texas, has come up with his own 10-point educational plan to combat innumeracy and illiteracy in the US. When someone pointed out that his plan actually only contained nine points, Mr Rains replied: 'You've just pointed your finger and emphasized the problem we're trying to resolve.'

Sunday Correspondent

'It's extremely dangerous to make predictions, especially about the future.'

UN representative, BBC Radio 4

A beefy newsagent stunned villagers when he turned up for work in a frock and told them: 'Call me Becky.' Then the 63-year-old Scots grandad handed out leaflets announcing his sex change and confessed: 'I have lived a lie all my life.' His devoted wife said: 'He always loved wearing kilts but I thought it was just because he was so proud of Scotland.'

People

In marked contrast to the conciliatory statements made by some hostages during their captivity in Beirut, several have called angrily for retaliation. 'Hunt 'em down, try 'em and kill 'em. It's that simple,' said Mr Peter Hill, aged 57, a guide for religious tours.

The Times

A squad of nature lovers who have been carrying toads across a busy road to their mating grounds in Yorkshire are being urged to hop it. For an unusually short breeding season means that numbers of toads who have finished mating and successfully recrossed the road on the way to marshes and dykes at Scarborough are being collected by the well-meaning patrol and carried back to Throxanby Mere. The frustrated toads then have to negotiate the main road yet again with an increased risk of being squashed by traffic.

Daily Telegraph

One of the pickets admits he went to daub 'Czech scab' on the man's house. 'But I couldn't spell Czech, so I wrote "Polish scab" instead,' he says.

Observer

THE COMMERCIAL BREAK

BOOK MARKETING COUNCIL

'John Craven's Children's Britain Comp.'
(Open to children in 3 age groups: 7 and under, 8–11, 12–161.)

Competitors' Journal

YOU LUCKY PEOPLE – FREE!

A fabulous football scarf for every reader. If you're football crazy, start the new season with flying colours – your favourite team's colours. In our latest, greatest offer, we are giving away a football scarf – worth £4.99 – FREE to every reader, so you can cheer on your team in style. Please enclose 2 x £1 coins or cheque/PO for each FREE scarf requested.

People

REPLICA 'DALEK' FOR SALE
Ex advert prop, full size, Patrick Troughton type. Grey body, silver balls and dome.

Doctor Who Appreciation Society newsletter

CRUEL AND UNUSUAL

He said a tribunal should sit on those sentenced to death, to be sure no mistake was being made.

Daily Telegraph

MAN FINED FOR BIRTH

Morning Star

THE COMPLETE BOOK
OF LOVE AND SEX
A Guide for all the Family
(ADULTS ONLY)

Book club ad

**In Chicago last week, a man out
shopping drew a gun and shot one of
two youths trying to rib him.**

Observer

Police in Cumbria are using fir trees to beat car thieves.

Independent

I was trying to find my ex-wife to give some legal papers to her – so I hired a private detective. But I began to worry about the sleuth's efficiency when he called on me three days later to see if I knew where she was.

News of the World

OH, REALLY?

'BLACK BASTARD' NOT RACIAL ABUSE, SAYS TRIBUNAL

Daily Telegraph

We sold 9,000 raffle tickets to raise money for renal research and nearly 3,000 donor cards were filled in. We even had some people offering to donate their kidneys there and then.

Unknown

Two bungling brothers tried to disguise themselves before setting off to rob a corner shop by blacking their faces with coal dust and wearing stocking masks. Their big mistake was to walk down a busy road in broad daylight.

News of the World

Transplanting carrots was always regarded as a recipe for disaster. But now three words have changed all that: cellular trays.

Organic Gardening

I've been having an affair with my boss, who insists that work is work and vice versa.

News of the World

Residents of Stow-on-the-Wold, Glos, took 10 days to realize that a new village sign read Stow-the-on-Wold. It has now been removed for repair.

Daily Telegraph

Recently the *Sunday Times* indulged in some top-people titillation by publishing lengthy reports on 'Sex, Love and Marriage' based on statistical surveys. Somewhat coyly, the paper announced the 'inexplicable oddity' that when political women were asked, 'Have you ever had sex with anyone besides your present partner?' one per cent of Conservative ladies responded by saying they did not know.

Tribune

The 3.15 race at Doncaster was named the Worth Laying Lady Riders' Handicap because it is being sponsored by a consortium of bookies. When the boob was pointed out, it was renamed simply the Worth Laying Handicap.

People

Mrs Thatcher pointed out several landmarks to ten-year-old Toby Blackledge from Bow, who sucked his orange lollipop and promised loyal support. He said afterwards, 'She stands for everything I believe in.'

Daily Telegraph

Seven deaf and dumb Japanese climbers were taken off 11,000ft Mt Cook last night by the New Zealand air force on the orders of Sir Robert Muldoon, the Prime Minister, because of avalanche dangers. Sir Robert said the climbers had talked to the mountain's chief ranger for two and a half hours and he didn't think they understood a word he said.

Daily Telegraph

A teenager swallowed four live goldfish at a village fair held to raise money for the RSPCA. Now angry officials are looking for the youth so they can prosecute.

People

A White House spokesman said yesterday that the Reagan Administration was following a policy of announcing nuclear tests only when they were considered 'significant'. Asked whether there was such a thing as a minor nuclear explosion, the spokesman, Larry Speakes, replied: 'Sure.'

Guardian

Paris: A young man survived a suicide attempt yesterday, but in the process killed two, injured thirteen and partially demolished a five-storey apartment house when he turned on gas jets in his kitchen, but then decided to have a last cigarette.

Independent

A new Wall Street Journal/NBC poll has discovered that for many Americans Ayatollah Khomeini is still the most unpopular Arab leader, notwithstanding the fact that he is dead – and not an Arab.

Independent

SACKED BALLET DANCER 'NOT MANLY ENOUGH'

Daily Telegraph

Of all the four-letter words in common parlance, 'fuck, cunt, mother-fucker and nigger' cause most offence, says the head of research of the Broadcasting Standards Council.

Morning Star

MASS MURDERER'S MENTAL HEALTH 'HAS DETERIORATED'

Evening Standard

New York's image as the crime capital of the world has been reinforced after a thief mugged a two-year-old monkey, recovering after a stroke, that was begging on the streets to pay off its medical bills.

Evening Standard

LITERALLY? I DON'T THINK SO

I pushed it hard and firmly into her. With a loud scream of ecstasy she literally exploded.

Men Only

He yanks me down for one last, final time and then explodes. His powerful jets trigger off my orgasm . . . and I literally melt within his firm grip. Somehow, shopping for lingerie will never be the same again.

Men Only

On the other hand, you can get pickled on *Woman's Hour* today – literally.

BBC Radio 4 trailer

Flying eye Bryan Woolfe stunned radio presenter Angela Rippon last night when he announced on air: 'I've been sacked.' Angela had just asked Bryan how the traffic was looking when he literally dropped a bomb-shell from his eye-in-the-sky helicopter.

Daily Mirror

OF CABBAGES AND THINGS

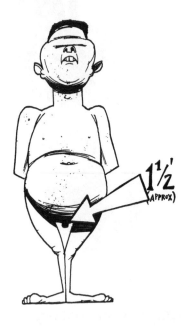

1½'
(APPROX)

Since they lost the war, Japanese people have been getting taller and taller, while Japanese things have been getting smaller and smaller.

Observer

Barbara Castle: 41 cauliflowers per minute destroyed.

Guardian

When Edwina Gateley went to the United States she told God: 'You pay the rent, you do the shopping, and I'll go and look for the prostitutes.'

TV Times

MP TO SEE COCKS ON SINN FEIN

Guardian

He turned his back on the Royal entourage, lifted his grass skirt and wiggled his bare and rather gaudily painted buttocks. However, the monarch's limousine flashed past without her seeing a thing, according to her aides.

Daily Telegraph

Young criminals are often portrayed as worthless layabouts who spend all their time in jail playing ping-pong or watching TV. Not true. From Stoke Heath Young Offender Institute, near Market Drayton, Shropshire, comes a letter revealing a sponsored press-up campaign at 1p a go to raise £10,000 for Marie Curie Cancer Care. Some of the lads have already heaved themselves up and down more than 10,000 times.

People

SHIRLEY THUT CARNT BEE WRITE?

The manager of a billiard hall was left snookered in the early hours of Tuesday – when he was hit over the head with a snooker cue. The 127-year-old man, from Hampstead, had tried to break up a dispute between two customers.

Camden New Journal

He was reported to have sought DM8 million in royalties on sales of Hitler's book *Mr in Kampf*.

The Times

Ms Merle Amory last night became the first black woman aged 28.

Guardian

The Red Crap Apple Tree. Bright red colours.

Advertising insert

Clinging to a chrome post in the middle of the carriage was a nun about 30 years old, dishevelled, red-faced, and totally catatonic with alcohol. The arrival of a 12-stone man in a bright red beret and mirror shades, surprisingly, did little to alleviate his anxiety.

Midweek

Borchardt is accused of disturbing the peace by hurling a choir against the window of the Turkish cultural centre.

Guardian

The Sing Sing chairs – otherwise known as 'Old Sparkies' – will not be taken out of mothballs, however. Instead, execution by lethal execution is proposed.

Independent

In a dawn commando-type ambush, shooting and creaming riot police set on miners' pickets and cars yesterday.

Morning Star

Made of 100% cotton indigo-dyed Denim. Garment washed by a specially developed process using Pumas.

Label on jeans

The admission that not all Labour MPs sharted at the bottom of the educational ladder was rather revealing.

Financial Times

EXCUSES, EXCUSES

A one-legged skiing instructor was cleared by magistrates yesterday of hitting a laughing policeman over the head with his artificial leg. Sgt Hulley admitted he laughed, but said this was not because of the man's disability, but because the false leg became stuck in his trousers, making it appear that he had a leg 8ft long.

Daily Telegraph

A man had the grin wiped off his face at Horseferry Road Court yesterday when he was fined £50 for giggling in the public gallery as a prison officer slipped off his chair. 'I wasn't giggling, I just sneezed,' he claimed.

Daily Telegraph

A woman accused of a $32,000 bank raid at Zion, Illinois, told police who arrested her after a high-speed car chase that her five-month-old son, asleep on the back seat, was there because 'I could not get a baby-sitter'.

Daily Telegraph

CRY FREEDOM!

Lawrence O'Dowd was fined £100 by York magistrates yesterday for saying 'Miaow' to a police dog. The unemployed 18-year-old was arrested in the centre of York and charged with using threatening and abusive words and behaviour. The court was told that O'Dowd was among a group of youngsters whom Sgt Taylor ordered to move on. As the officer approached, O'Dowd miaowed. Sgt Taylor said that, in the situation, he regarded the word 'miaow' as abusive.

Guardian

A man who was kicked in the face by a police officer was then charged with causing criminal damage to his boot, a court heard yesterday.

Morning Star

Firemen in South Yorkshire have been told to pretend to squirt their hoses in training to save on water bills.

Independent

Jim Mosely has just been pardoned after serving nearly two years of a five-year prison sentence in Georgia, USA. His crime, which he mistakenly revealed in his 1988 divorce hearing, was to have oral sex with his wife, Betty. 'Oral sex has been illegal here since 1865,' said Clive Stafford Smith, the British lawyer who had the important but rather embarrassing job of defending Mr Mosely. A few days ago Mr Stafford Smith told me the basis of his successful appeal. 'In Georgia, the crimes of bestiality, public obscenity and necrophilia all carry lighter sentences. I informed the court that if my client had committed an indecent act with a dead donkey in the middle of town, he would have got a shorter prison sentence.'

Sunday Correspondent

OSCAR WILDE, EAT YOUR HEART OUT

I further resent being referred to as a stooge but I shall resist the temptation to call Mr Paysley-Tyler a jumped-up twerp because I feel the debate on this very serious subject should be kept above the level of personal abuse.

Camden New Journal

The woman stood about five feet eight and while she was beautifully proportioned she was colossal. To say that she was built like a brick shit-house just would not do her justice.

Mayfair

The harrowing story of a girl in the grip of anorexia. 'Terrific! I devoured it at one sitting' — Fay Weldon.

Book club catalogue

After having read Rose Sheperd's delightful interview with Mike McShane, which ended with Mr McShane's remark that Ms Sheperd was the first interviewer not to make gratuitous mention of his size, I was disappointed that you saw fit to print the caption, 'American Whale' under Mr McShane's picture.

Independent

A vicar ended a sermon on sin by warning his stunned flock: 'And if you don't stop talking about me and the churchwarden I won't give you communion.' The father of four added: 'If I were a Moslem I could wish that your fingernails fall out.'

Daily Mirror

YOUR WIFE'S SO UGLY SHE NEEDS A BAG ON HER HEAD – SAYS CLEANER SALESMAN

Daily Mirror

QUITE RIGHT, TOO

POLICE TO CURB USE OF TOILETS FOR SEX

Pinner Leader

A jobless skinhead who hurled a rotten egg at the Prime Minister, and missed, was fined £50 yesterday.

Daily Telegraph

TEBBIT VICTIMS 'WILL RECEIVE COMPENSATION'

Morning Star

Cosmetics to improve the beauty of cows has got to stop, British farmers have been told.

Costa Blanca News

It is difficult to write a dull book about Disraeli, and Jane Ridley hasn't even tried.

New Statesman

Thanks to all the would-be Brigitte Bardots who have written in following my story about the mini-TV series being made about her life. I have passed your letters and pictures to the film company – with the exception of that from Harold of Bromsgrove.

Sunday Mirror

AGENTS PORTRAYED HITLER AS GAY JEWISH EUNUCH

Independent

A man who turned up to a stately home wearing a pair of large pink plastic buttocks was bound over by a Harrogate court. During the case, the buttocks were kept in a paper bag and were not shown to magistrates.

Morning Star

WOULD YOU CARE TO REPHRASE THAT?

'I decided to paint my water-butt to blend in with the house and surrounding plants, using oil-based paints left over from jobs around the house,' writes Karen. I'm inspired by what Karen has achieved, and I hope you are – if you've got a glorious butt you'd like to show off, send me a photo!

Garden Answers

Now, *The Archers* – and David and Ruth are recovering from a hard day's combining.

Radio 4

Have any readers got a record-breaking bush? Send me a photo.

Garden Answers

Looking for a hero: modern comic-book characters toil in an imperfect world. Plus, shaving bad compact discs and pumping gas from Uranus.

Omni

Rainsaver. All you need to channel rainwater
– without your Butt flooding when full.

Advertising insert

**The memorandum also said that the
litre was now 'overwhelmingly the unit
for petrol retailing' and that the rule
demanding display of the price of a
gallon would be scrapped. Mr Kenneth
Warren (C, Hastings and Rye),
committee chairman, said the decision
would cause confusion. 'We just think
that if you like to drink bitter in pints
why should you not have petrol in
gallons?'**

Daily Telegraph

TV CHIEF TO PUT FINGER IN DYKE

Morning Star

DYKE GETS FINGER OUT

Independent

East Germany is selling 1,500 Rottweiler and Alsatian dogs once used to guard the border with the West. 'The dogs are not man-eaters at all. They like children.'

Independent

Deborah was so keen on her four-legged friend that she took horse nuts in her pocket to the Camden School for Girls and would sniff them.

People

A number of women protestors against Trident have made statements alleging that their underclothes were removed. They say they were forced to undergo full body searches at two Strathclyde police stations while men looked on. A spokesman for Strathclyde police in Glasgow yesterday confirmed that an inquiry would be held. It is understood it will be an internal one.

Guardian

POLICE HELPLESS AT DRUG PARTY

Daily Telegraph

It is issuing the following advice to parents: 'Do not let anyone into your home until you have checked their identity. If you are unsure ring the social services department's children's division. Report all suspicious callers to the police immediately and do not let them enter your home.'
JIMMY GREAVES IS ON HOLIDAY.

Harrow Independent

Jenny, from Norwich, says: 'Attitudes to sex have changed. My generation is freer about it – we are a product of the pill.'

News of the World

Clary was shunned by TV bosses three months ago after suggesting in front of thirteen million viewers that he had performed a perverted sex act with former Chancellor Norman Lamont. Producer Michael Hurll said: 'There is no way he would do such a thing again. But we are taking no chances. His spot is being taped.'

Daily Mirror

A top doctor, backing the warning last night, said: 'Teenagers in particular need to be careful. Hot sticky discos are the sort of places where illness spreads. The best advice is to stick to one partner.'

People

A resident of the Hereford and Worcester hamlet of Callow Hill, near Bewdley, claims he is being disturbed by a noise from a game usually associated with Gauloise-scented village squares in France. He has written to Wyre Forest District Council to complain about *pétanque* players 'shouting and clacking their balls and groaning'.

Independent

Farmer Geoff Hardy, of Ingoldmells, Lincs, is to sleep with 30 pigs to raise charity cash.

Daily Mirror

Later President Reagan's campaign chief apologized for the president's remark that the choice of Ms Ferraro might be 'the biggest bust politically in recent history'.

The Times

Bare-breasted Lynda Purvis bounced into the ring to help him celebrate his victory. 'The wrestler thought she was getting all the cheers, which she was, and they started an argument that went all the way back to the dressing-room.' There manager Dennis Lord tried to calm them down. 'But it was obvious they had fallen out for good.'

News of the World

Mr Methane, a folk hero in his home town of Macclesfield and a minor cult figure as far away as Buxton, has failed to persuade insurance companies to provide cover for his most valuable asset. He is able to pass wind in time and in tune with a selection of modern and classical pieces and is particularly in demand for performances of 'Happy Birthday to You' at birthday parties. He said: 'If they could insure Liberace's hands, Betty Grable's legs and Samantha Fox's breasts, why not my derrière? It is my bread and butter.'

Independent

The British Standard Institute is best-known for its kitemark often found on condom machines: 'This product was tested to BSI 3704.' 'So was the Titanic,' runs the joke. Yet it is only one of 10,000 BSI standards that relate to the worthiness of products ranging from screws to ships.

Independent

FROM BEYOND THE GRAVE

CANNIBAL VICTIMS SPEAK OUT

Independent

> A year after her death, Jackie Kennedy Onassis is setting the style for the New York spring.

Daily Telegraph

HEADLESS CORPSE WAS TOURIST FROM NIGERIA

The Times

MOTHER LEFT FORTUNE TO HER DEAD SON

Evening Standard

Freed killers and rapists could soon be banned by law from returning to haunt their victims.

People

A pensioner was outraged when a mail order firm named his wife Shopper of the Year ... 13 years after her death. The newspaper-style leaflets also dubbed her an 'agony aunt' and urged people to write to her for tips on how to pick up bargain buys.

News of the World

September 18, 1970, is a date not unknown to most people as it marks the untimely death of the original guitar hero, Jimi Hendrix. On February 28, 1986, Polydor Records are releasing 'Jimi at Monterrey', an album recorded at the Monterrey Festival in 1976.

Hampstead Advertiser

A lawyer asked a Los Angeles judge yesterday to sentence a dead man to life imprisonment.

Daily Telegraph

Back from the dead – John Fagan meets the late Pope Paul.

Sunday Mirror

After his death, Estelle and Francois were married.

Tammy

A family of three were seriously ill in hospital last night after being found unconscious by their dead pet dog.

People

The Wimbledon Committee for Central America has an unusual object for sale at its fair in St Mark's Place, SW19, a week on Saturday. Among the cakes, pottery and old books will be Ronald Reagan's missing brain.

Evening Standard

DENTISTS CONTINUE WORKING DESPITE PATIENTS' DEATHS

The Times

MISSING MAN 'FOUND IN TOMB'

People

TOO GOOD TO BE TRUE?

WHOOMP

Mrs Rosalind Runcie, wife of the Archbishop of Canterbury, had trouble with the wind after she lit a candle in Covent Garden, London, yesterday.

Guardian

A club committee member said some people with Mrs MacWilliams had had their membership suspended for three months for their behaviour that night. He said these included the man who had his trousers and pants pulled down for photographs, Mr Dick Hampton.

Evening Standard

After 35 years, Miller's play *Death of a Salesman* is back on Broadway. Bigsby asked the playwright what different actors had brought to the celebrated part of Willy Loman. 'There were three really. One was Warren Mitchell, who played it marvellously in London. His Willy and Dustin Hoffman's are related. They are both small fellows ... Probably Dustin's is the most lucid of all the Willies I'm aware of.'

The Listener and Radio 4

In the meantime vegetarians should head for the Ajimura in Covent Garden, where there is a vegetarian set lunch for £7.70. And you will have the healthiest, NACNE approved, stools in London.

Guardian

He then roused himself into a quite terrific climax in the O-level version of M. Mitterrand's language. '*Vive le France!*' he roared.

Daily Telegraph

Dave was in good form, hitting a 180 and then following up with 2 tons. Neil was unlucky in his singles when Paul broke his shaft midway through the game.

Darts league newsletter

HEDGEHOG'S 300-MILE CAR CHASE

Daily Mirror

BLACK COCK CASTS A SHADOW OVER THE NEW DAWN

Observer

GULF EGGS PUT WIND UP UK PRODUCERS

Guardian

MICKEY MOUSE AIDS REAGAN IN LAUNCHING TAX REFORM PLAN

Daily Telegraph

A chimpanzee called Sammy who escaped from Belgrade Zoo and went looking for a mate was arrested as he tried to enter a cinema without a ticket.

Daily Telegraph

MAD COW FAMILIES WILL SUE

Daily Mirror

'NO DANGER IF YOU DON'T BREATHE'

Morning Star

Supermarket trolleys come in all shapes and sizes, but they have never lost their wanderlust: I have heard of people using them to wheel their tools around in, for instance.

You & Yours, BBC Radio 4

CALL FOR SHOPS TO SELL HEARING AIDS 'JUST LIKE BEANS'

Daily Telegraph

BOTTOM CLUBS GIVING THEMSELVES AIRS

Daily Telegraph

The man, who admitted the robbery, was caught because staff at the building society recognized him as a regular customer. He was wearing a joke mask with a large nose and big rubbery lips.

Daily Telegraph

BOOK REVIEWS: *Making Sense of English in Religion* by Laurence Twaddle.

Writing Magazine

DOCTOR RACES WOODLICE

Daily Telegraph

DEAR SIR,
I AM NOT MAD,
YOURS SINCERELY . . .

The huge wrestler Giant Haystacks is welcome to tea at my place any time – even though he might eat up a month's housekeeping. I'd lay on a massive spread, and then when he was in a good mood I'd get him to jump on my neighbour.

News of the World

My wife likes Roger Moore, so if we were neighbours I could laugh and shout: 'Fancy you being a millionaire and living in a council house!'

News of the World

My 13-year-old son was mad keen to buy a dog, but I wasn't in case I was the one who had to take it for walks. But he's a good persuader. He bought a collar and lead and went down the street dragging it along and saying to an imaginary pet: 'Come on, Rover. Good boy.' I was so worried what the neighbours would think that I've agreed to buy him a dog.

News of the World

Mary Kenny is right in asserting that mothers with small children receive little sympathy or concern from the general public. My advice to any young mother hoping for consideration on the London Underground would be to disguise her children as dogs.

Sunday Telegraph

YUK!

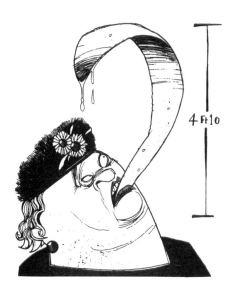

4 Ft 10

Q. What can I do with my mother-in-law's tongue, which is 4ft 10in high and has to lean against the wall for support?

People

NEIGHBOUR ACQUITTED OF DUMPING ENTRAILS

Independent

LABOUR PLANS TO EXTRACT EGGS EVIDENCE FROM CURRIE

Daily Telegraph

PEER'S WIFE BURNED AT BARBECUE

Sunday Telegraph

For seven and a half years I've worked alongside him, and I'm proud to be his partner. We've had triumphs, we've made mistakes, we've had sex.' This was George Bush describing his relationship with President Reagan, at the College of Southern Idaho on May 6.

New Statesman

Scarborough has been judged the most convenient resort in the country, providing one lavatory for every 550 inhabitants.

Daily Telegraph

The Prime Minister brought in some new faces to her cabinet tonight and re-arranged some others.

ITN News at Ten

A German whose penis was cut off by his girlfriend has auctioned it in Frankfurt for £40 and a bottle of schnapps.

Daily Mirror

But you do not have to have a formal lily pond – there can be equal pleasure in sitting beside a 'wildlife' pond. You can become absorbed in the darting visits of dragonflies, the antics of the pond skaters, and the occasional mysterious 'plop'.

Organic Gardening

Instead of counting sheep insomniacs should consider sleeping with them according to researchers at Hull University.

Big Issue

SPIDER RAPIST STRIKES AGAIN

Unknown

HUH??

ELF GETS ORKNEY COUNCIL HANDOUT

Morning Star

The Soviet Union under Mr Andropov is returning to a narrow Stalinist type of government at the Lyric Theatre, Hammersmith.

Guardian

BURGLAR HID IN SOFA FOR A YEAR

Daily Telegraph

YORKSHIRE MIGHT HAVE BEEN ATOM BOMB TEST SITE

The Times

In a magazine interview Sagawa said what he most needed now was 'a real woman's love' and that his cannibalism was 'an expression of love'. He said the thing to be most careful of in future relations with women was 'not to eat them'.

Observer

GOODBYE TO THE FLUSH TOILET
We have for sale a BIO LOO (no water required). Not a chemical toilet. Up to 4 full-time persons or 10 part-time.

Organic Gardening

Postman Pat may be banned from Japan ... because of his Mafia links.

Daily Mirror

TARZAN IS IRA TARGET

News of the World

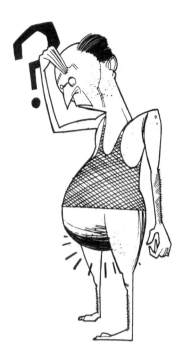

'PENIS' MISSING

Independent

Several hundred punk rockers rampaged through Hanover over the weekend, battling with German police, urinating in unison and threatening to lay waste the city.

Independent

BAKKABAKK....KA

WEASEL JAILED FOR GUN FURY

Daily Mirror

THE RECORD BREAKERS

Ten armed men broke into a cheese factory in Parma, Italy, yesterday and escaped with £210,000 worth of Parmesan cheese. Police claimed it was the greatest cheese robbery in history.

Daily Telegraph

A RECORD YEAR FOR CRUMPETS

Britain ate its way through a record 860 million crumpets in the past 12 months and the industry is now worth £37 million a year, according to a survey published yesterday. But crumpets remain relatively unpopular in Scotland.

Morning Star

HOLD PAGE 2!

PILCHARDS WEREN'T KILLERS

People

ANTI-PORK VOTE IN JERUSALEM

The Times

ALCOHOLICS 'MUST STAY OFF DRINK'

Daily Telegraph

KILLER DOGS 'VERY MEAN BUNCH'

Morning Star

THE POPE PATS A RHINO

Sunday Telegraph

THE POOR – THEY SUFFER

Economist

THE VICTIM ALSO SUFFERS

Economist

OH WELL, THAT'S OK THEN

Mr Jameson was recalled to the witness box to answer questions about the pictures. He denied that they were all nudes. He said: 'One of them is wearing a top hat.'

Daily Telegraph

Two ambulancemen who stopped to buy fish and chips on the way to a hospital with an emergency heart patient have been dismissed for gross misconduct. The ambulancemen said the patient had given them permission.

Guardian

Britain's nuclear defences are down ... and that's official. For sub-postmaster Tony Brown hasn't got the football rattle he is meant to sound to warn villagers if attack is imminent. A Home Office spokesman for the UK warning and monitoring HQ in Oxford said: 'If war looked imminent we would issue him with a new rattle.'

Sunday Mirror

People are very narrow-minded. They say I've had scores of teenage lovers, but they're wrong. I've kept count of them all and there have been only 15 or 20.

News of the World

They were found guilty of drinking on duty, neglect of duty and disobeying orders, but were cleared of the more serious charge of discreditable conduct. Both police officers plan to appeal. PC Edwin said: 'I think it is a harsh sentence and we are both going to appeal. After all, all we were doing was what we are trained to do, and that's use initiative.'

Evening Standard

Q. I'm fourteen and one of my boobs is smaller than the other. Does it matter?
A. Be positive. Say that one is bigger than the other.

People

Augusto Pinochet, the Chilean army chief, said he never meant to offend the West German army when he referred to it on Wednesday as a corps composed of 'marijuana smokers, drug addicts, long-hairs, homosexuals and unionists'.

Independent

Disgusted parents have slammed a best-selling talking book, based on the blockbuster _Lion King_ movie, which appears to give children some very fruity advice. Press the button alongside the picture of baboon Rifiki and out comes what sounds for all the world like: 'Squashed bananas up your a**e.' And that's the vulgar slogan millions of kids could be aping this Christmas. Parents who complain about the popular stocking filler are told by the publishers that the phrase is actually 'Arsanti sana' – Swahili for 'You're a baboon and I'm not!'

People

An electrical fault in an old metal lamppost in Brighton killed a dog when he received a shock after answering the call of nature in the time-honoured doggy way. The lights in the whole street were put out of action while electricity board engineers repaired the fault. East Sussex county council, which owns the lampposts, is investigating to see whether other dogs could be faced with a similar hazard. A spokesperson for the council said: 'There is no danger to humans. Animals have a much lower resistance to electric shocks than we do.'

Public Service

Last month Shirley Williams told supporters in Birmingham: 'The people of Birmingham have not had to suffer from the kind of Labour extremism that people in Sandwell and Walsall have faced.' Liberals campaigning in Birmingham (mis)quoted Williams as saying 'The people of Birmingham have had to suffer . . .' Liberal candidate Graham Gopsill explained: 'We didn't agree with her, so we took out the word "not" . . . Shirley Williams had been making a speech about extremists. That was the point.'

Labour Weekly

'People think we used to run a knocking shop,' she said. 'But it was a respectable massage parlour which provided hand relief if requested.'

News of the World

FAIR ENOUGH

HOSPITAL BAN ON SURGEON'S GUIDE DOG

Daily Telegraph

Nearly all of South Glamorgan's ambulances were taken off the road last night, because their back wheels keep falling off.

Daily Telegraph

A home computer, a liking for chess and a broader view of the world have conspired to make Dave 'the thinking man's darts player'. Dave is a reclusive figure at the Lakeside, and on his home turf at the El Dorado Club, Clacton, where, it is said, the locals have learned to leave him alone as he throws up.

Sunday Times

The Lancashire town of Burnley went into a state of nuclear alert last week when civil defence sirens housed in the local police station were let off. At least, it would have done if anyone had taken any notice.

Tribune

The average Londoner eats 20lb of chocolate a year. If, after gorging on free samples, you still feel you are falling behind, there may yet be time to grab a cab to a serious chocolate shop and buy a pound of your favourite centres. If you happen to be the Queen Mother, the first stop will be Charbonnel et Walker, for a hundredweight of rose and violet creams – doubtless chosen because they don't show when she dribbles violet fondant down her front.

Independent

Prince Charles has been invited to join Italy's Ugly Club because of his romance with Camilla Parker Bowles.

People

A fight between two elderly room-mates in an old folks' home landed one of them in hospital with a fractured pelvis. They had to be separated by staff, but not before an 84-year-old man had knocked his 96-year-old room-mate to the floor. Acting Detective Constable Stephen Dower said: 'We don't know what caused the fight, but at that age they often don't know either.'

Ruislip Recorder

A large television audience in Houston, Texas, was taken aback to hear one of the leading candidates in the mayoral race say, over what he thought was a dead microphone, that the only way to control the spread of AIDS was to 'shoot the queers'. 'I apologize, but I don't think I had the gay vote anyway,' he said later.

Unknown

... AND WE APOLOGIZE FOR ANY EMBARRASSMENT CAUSED

Due to a transcription error, an article in Saturday's *Independent* on page 2 on Irish premier Charles Haughey mistakenly read 'a man of charm and immense rudeness'. This was intended to read 'a man of charm and great shrewdness'.

Independent

Yesterday we incorrectly recorded that up to 200 late-night revellers 'danced in drag' after time at the Willows Club in Netherton. The sentence should have read that the revellers 'danced and drank' after time. We apologize for this mistake.

Wolverhampton Express and Star

We regret that Wednesday's article on Molesworth stated that the protest was to be 'ignored' by peace movement leaders from other European countries. The sentence should have read 'tomorrow's protest will be joined by ...'

Morning Star

The caption to the photograph of the Freedom Farrowing System on page 2 yesterday said it was developed with aid from the NSPCC. It should have read the RSPCA.

Independent

On 18 September we published a report stating that Suzi Quatro has been secretly in love with Gary Glitter for three months. This story was totally incorrect. Suzi, who was not contacted by us before we published the report, has told us that she has only seen Gary Glitter on one occasion in the last 10 years and that was at a recent business meeting at his manager's office.

Daily Mirror

Jim White's reference to George Michael's first contact with the law incorrectly stated that a judge released him from his record contract, expressing shock at its terms. In fact, the problem was ultimately resolved by mutual agreement and there was no occasion on which a judge released Mr Michael from his contract and expressed shock at its contents. We apologize for any confusion caused by the error. The contract was described as having all the mutual benefits of one drawn up by a Mafia don. The Mafia of course had nothing to do with the matter.

Independent

In the August 8 edition, a photo of famed Nazi hunter Simon Wiesenthal was incorrectly identified as Dr Josef Mengele. We regret the error.

Weekly World News

ACCOUNTING ASSISTANTS
Keen to broaden your experience?
c£12,000
Chevron welcomes sex with all suitably disabled people regardless of size of bank balance.

Evening Standard

AN APOLOGY

In Monday's *Evening Standard* an advertisement appeared in the recruitment pages for Accounting Assistants for Chevron UK Ltd. Unfortunately the ad included a closing line which was by nature very offensive and possibly damaging to Chevron, Bernard Hodes Advertising, and the *Evening Standard*. It also, no doubt, caused some great offence to the *Evening Standard* readers. We would like to make clear that the inclusion of this line has nothing to do with either Chevron or Bernard Hodes or the *Evening Standard*. As the artwork studio who created this advertisement we have to accept full responsibility for its appearance – however we would like to state quite clearly that it was not an intentional or malicious act and most definitely should not have appeared. Once again our apologies to all concerned.

Evening Standard

The Times was quick yesterday to correct its contention that Tim Renton, the new Minister of State at the Foreign Office, was once Great Uncle Bulgaria in *The Wombles*. For those who missed it, the paper noted with considerable restraint: 'The statement that he once held a position in the entertainment industry was incorrect.'

Daily Telegraph

Horn Abbot International Limited, the maker of the game Trivial Pursuit, wish to apologize to the Rt. Hon. Kenneth Clarke, QC, MP, for the inclusion in one of the editions of the game of the following question and answer:
Q. Which health minister thought that coloured immigrants came from Bongo-Bongo Land?
A. Kenneth Clarke.
Horn Abbot International Limited wish to make it clear that they entirely accept that Mr Clarke was not the author of the remark to which the question alludes and that he has never held or expressed any such views. At Mr Clarke's request, a payment has been made to a charity of his choice.

Newspaper ad

In our June issue we said that Ra Bonewitz, the trance medium and psychic who works with crystals, has been a basketball star and is now a monk. This is not true, and we apologize. He has in fact been a helicopter test pilot and a geologist with the US Atomic Energy Commission.

New Health

We inadvertently printed a sentence of *Dreams From the Strangers' Café Guidelines* as ' . . . although any old crap will be accepted.' This should of course read ' . . . although NOT any old crap will be accepted.'

Zene

WHAA...???

HIDEOUS GRIN HUNTED

Morning Star

Cardiff has moved 40 miles closer to London, according to an official Government handbook on Britain.

Sunday Mirror

300 BATS REVIVE DRUNKEN PATIENT

Daily Telegraph

One hundred firemen fought a huge blaze at a parcel sorting office in east London. The first two floors of the Parcel Force building in Stephenson Street, Canning Town, east London, were extensively damaged but the parcels escaped.

ITV Teletext

HOUSE GUESTS PACKED IN TIN

Camden New Journal

A 21-year-old man has been arrested after allegedly trying to sexually assault Minnie Mouse at the Disneyland disco near Los Angeles.

Evening Standard

78 SNAILS BEATEN BY HERCULES

Daily Telegraph

BRIDGE STUNT TURKEY MIMIC ACQUITTED

Daily Telegraph

ANGRY NUDISTS STRIP POLICE

Daily Telegraph

THE DAY THE VICAR BEGAN TO BARK

Sunday Times

Golliwogs have been banned from Islington town hall – after sneaking in on bicycles.

Evening Standard

'BAN CHURCH WEDDINGS' PLEA BY VICARS

Sunday Mirror

NO REGRETS, SAY HIPPO-EATERS

Daily Telegraph

MAN BITTEN BY BATHTUB SEAL

Daily Telegraph

ARCHITECT WAS BEATEN WITH FRENCH LOAF

Daily Telegraph

DISCOUNT IF YOU'RE BURIED AT A TILT

Daily Telegraph

ACCUSED MAN TO GET LEG BACK

Daily Telegraph

GIANT TORTOISE PIG-OUT

Independent

BRAINS TEST HAMSTERS FLEE

Daily Telegraph

WRINKLE-FREE TOMATO MUST NOT BE EATEN

Daily Telegraph

REALLY? THAT'S, ER, VERY INTERESTING

MY HEAD WAS A MARSHMALLOW FOR 12 WEEKS

Daily Mirror

I MET CHRIST AS A BIG FLUFFY DONKEY

Independent

My husband came back from the pub and went to bed. Later I took him a cup of tea, but as he had the bedclothes over his head I let him sleep on. But when I went to bed myself I was surprised to find he had turned into a bear.

News of the World

Small people are urgently needed by residents in Twerton.

Bath Chronicle

Britain's most useless man is living in Ruislip.

Ruislip Recorder

Liz and I don't like the word lesbian and don't feel our sexuality is anybody's business but our own. We call ourselves a 'functional parenting pair bond unit'.

Independent

MORE SCOTS STAY IN SCOTLAND

Daily Telegraph

THE HISTORY OF LAUNDRY (4000BC–1950)

Collaborator urgently required to help complete editing lifetime's research.

Writers' Monthly

NO ANIMAL HAS HORNS WHICH GROW TO SIX THOUSAND TIMES THEIR LENGTH IN FORTY YEARS

Guardian

DOES THIS REALLY SOUND LIKELY?

It also emerged last week that Miss Gabor's driving licence had been altered in ballpoint pen. She explained that the licence was stolen by 'Mexicans' who thoughtfully returned it with her age and weight reduced.

Independent

CHRIST IS YORKSHIREMAN

Daily Telegraph

DOG BLAMED FOR BURNING HOUSE DOWN

The fire brigade yesterday blamed a house fire on a dog playing with matches.

Morning Star

Research has shown that mice that drink green tea are 40 per cent less likely to develop skin cancers.

Daily Mirror

A man buzzed by a low-flying plane made a down-to-earth reply with his lawnmower. Angry Peter Hornby, 60, cut 20ft letters in a field. His message to the pilot he believed had come from nearby Oaksey, Wilts, was: 'F— off Oksy.' His wife Pru, 49, explained: 'He wrote Oksy instead of spelling out Oaksey because he got tired.'

Daily Mirror

YOU DON'T SAY

The ancient Japanese ceremony of bowing can kill. Courtesy has cost at least 24 people their lives in Tokyo – 12 of them after accidentally hitting their heads together and being knocked under trains and buses.

Daily Mirror

A Hillary Clinton look-alike who worked as a stripper in Potsdam, Germany, has given up her act. Hardly anyone came to see the show.

People

The imitation duck calls made by Dimitris Thomasinas to lure birds his way when he went shooting in Salonika at the weekend were so lifelike that two of his colleagues fired at the bushes where he was hiding and shot him dead. Deaths and injuries among Greeks who go shooting are said by their association to be taking on serious proportions.

Daily Telegraph

He claimed he was the reincarnated brother of Conan the Barbarian, that he was turning into an elk and had played for Leeds United. A defence psychiatrist said he was mad.

Daily Telegraph

SATANIST REFUSED TO REPAIR CHURCH

Daily Telegraph

A pub menu offering King Herod Baby Burgers and Crucified Kippers was branded tasteless by a local priest in Studley, Warwicks.

Daily Mirror

The idea that samples of inflatable sex dolls should be placed in their library caused hilarity in the Lords when Lord Barnett suggested it.

Daily Telegraph

NO SELLOTAPING PUPILS' MOUTHS, SCHOOL TOLD

Daily Telegraph

A woman can be distinguished from a herring gull by the fact that, when feeding her young, she does not regurgitate half-digested fish.

Guardian

Voracious toads the size of dinner plates are hitchhiking across Northern Australia gobbling up wildlife – and officials are appealing to motorists not to give them lifts.

Evening Standard

DISARMAMENT PROGRESS WAS 'BAULKED BY WARS'

Ham and High

Picnics are boring because the food chosen is unimaginative, a Gallup Poll report claimed yesterday.

Daily Telegraph

The dead mouse arrived last Tuesday. The package was stinking and blood had seaped through it. It had been placed in another envelope bearing a Post Office sticker: 'Package damaged in post.'

Morning Star

WOMEN ARE NOW VISIBLE

Public Service

STORIES I WISH I'D READ

THIEVES EAT ZOO

Daily Mirror

EXPLODING HEAD SYNDROME QUITE HARMLESS

Daily Telegraph

THE SICK MAN OF EUROPE WHO INVADED AN ARAB BLANCMANGE

Daily Telegraph

ACCUSED MAN 'DEVOURED HIS OWN TROUSERS'

Daily Telegraph

THE EXORCIST VICAR DECIDES TO BANISH TODDLERS' PLAYGROUP

Camden New Journal

NUDE PIANIST THOUGHT HE WAS GOD

Hampstead Advertiser

BOY BEHEADED TO WIN A PRIZE

Evening Standard

RHINO VOYAGES HALF WAY ROUND WORLD

Daily Telegraph

UK DISAPPEARING

Observer

JAIL EX-WIFE PLEA BY WOMBLE

Daily Telegraph

THE EXPLOSION AFTER THE LOBSTER

Tribune

UNDERWEAR 'HAVOC' IN HIGH STREET

Camden New Journal

KILLER SHRIMP POUNCES AT 30ft A SECOND

Daily Telegraph

PYJAMAS TO STOP TRAFFIC

Morning Star

2ft SURPRISE FOR 5ft WOMAN

Morning Star

WOMBLE IN LOVE SPLIT

News of the World

ARMY PROBE FAILS TO FIND NAZI PLANTS

Unknown

HOLD THE FRONT PAGE!

SCIENTISTS SEE END IN SIGHT FOR SQUISHY TOMATOES

Squishy tomatoes may soon be a thing of the past, thanks to British scientists.

Daily Telegraph

SHEEP TO BE DIPPED

Guardian

MP DISCOVERS 'NO CHANGE' IN RUSSIAN MUD

Daily Telegraph

SHOPKEEPERS 'NOT TO BLAME FOR SNIFFING'

Daily Telegraph

POLICE CONFUSED BY 'ABSOLUTELY NOTHING'

Holborn Guardian

LEAVE CANCELLED IN NUCLEAR WAR, HOSPITAL STAFF TOLD

Ham and High

HANDSHAKE CHAOS

Guardian

RATEPAYER WINS RIGHT TO PUT RUBBISH IN DUSTBINS

Daily Telegraph

SO WHAT ELSE IS NEW?

STUDENTS TO HIGHLIGHT NEED FOR BATHS

Morning Star

Corpses may soon be eligible for degrees at Cambridge University.

The Times

One of the world's most prestigious computer-based energy prediction models – one which has held the attention of governments and been widely used by energy lobbies throughout the Western world and maybe even in Russia – has suddenly been shown to be a load of old rubbish.

Guardian

DEAR SIR

SIR, I recently saw a window sticker produced by the National Union of Teachers proclaiming: 'If you can read this thank a teacher.' Could someone advise me who I should thank if, like increasing numbers of school leavers today, I could *not* read it?

Daily Telegraph

Sir, There's only one way to deal with dog rapists who come before the courts. Give 'em the cat!

Guardian

WHAT'S ON NEXT

12.15 p.m. Stereo
The Ones That Got Away
Andrew Huth examines one or two things you've been spared recently.

Radio Times